Beautiful, Strong Women

Poems of the Journey to Overcoming Domestic Violence

By
Kimberly Hockaday

Copyright © 2018 Kimberly Hockaday
Published by K.I.M. Publishing, 2018

The author asserts the moral right under the Copyright, Designs and Patents Act 1988 to be identified as the author of this work.

All rights reserved. No part of this publication may be reproduced, stored in a retrieval system, or transmitted, in any form or by any means without the prior written consent of the author, nor be otherwise circulated in any form of binding or cover other than that in which it is published and without a similar condition being imposed on the subsequent purchaser.

Dedication

To the women who have made it out of an abusive relationship:

Remember.
But do not linger
Into the past.
You are now stronger.
Wiser.
A SURVIVOR!

To the women who are still in an abusive relationship:

May God give you strength.
Clarity.
The courage.
TO BREAK FREE.

Contents

Introduction 1

All She Wants 3

When? 4

Burning Flame 5

Troubled Waters 6

The Other You 7

Mirror, Mirror 8

The Past 10

Bruised, not Broken 11

If People Knew Me 12

He Saved Me 13

Accept Me 14

I Dance 15

She Wears a Smile 16

Judge Me Not 17

Bruises Fade 18

When I Think of Him 19

What Would You Say? 20

To My Younger Self 21

Baggage 22

I'm Real 24

Words of Wisdom 25

Reflection 26

I Am a Woman 27

You Don't Know Me 28

My Guidance 29

Going to Make It 30

Why Do We Love People? 31

Lost 32

You Are so Beautiful 33

Odd Girl Out 34

Perfection She Never Claimed to Be 35

Trying to Live 36

Silence 37

Behind the Mask 38

Who Are We 39

Need of Love 40

- Lost and Confused 42
- Lost Now Found 43
- She Fell in Love with a Man 44
- He Loves Me 46
- Help Me 47
- The Darkness 48
- See Me 49
- One Day 50
- Wallflower Child 51
- Escape 52
- Love Me or Leave Me 53
- The Fear 54
- Before It's Physical 55
- Black Butterfly 56
- The Son, the Father 57
- You Don't Love Me 58
- Unbreakable 59
- Rainbow Spirit 60
- Let Go 61
- You Can Do It 62
- Until It's Too Late 63

Call Now 64

One Day at a Time 65

Stronger 66

Life is Beautiful 67

Let us not Forget 68

Beautiful, Strong Woman 69

Rise Up! 70

Sisters United 72

Contact the Author 74

Acknowledgments 75

Further Books from the Author 76

About the Author 77

State Coalitions 78

Introduction

The world is filled with so many problems, one of which is close to my heart — Domestic Violence. Every day, thousands of women are beaten, living in fear, and ashamed to let anyone know. Some of these women are lucky enough to make it out, but, unfortunately, many have lost their lives.

This book was written to be the voice for the women who are too afraid to speak, to celebrate the women who have the strength to walk away, and also to memorialize all the women who lost their lives to Domestic Violence. This terrible, deep, dark secret must be brought into public focus. It has to stop.

I hope this book brings hope and shines a light on Domestic Violence to help make a difference in the lives of those who do not really understand what it is.

My desire is that every woman who reads this book can find inspiration and know their true worth.

If you are a victim, or if you know someone who is in need of help, please call the National Domestic Violence Hotline, 1-800-799-7233. You can also find more information in the back of the book. If you are reading this outside the USA, then please contact your local helpline.

All She Wants

She just wants a hug.
To simply be embraced.
To feel a sense of belonging,
Somewhere some place.
But she tells no one
Of what she is feeling.
Because they would make fun of her
And accuse her of attention seeking.
But she knows that a hug
Would squeeze the pain inside her away.
Reassuring her that she is loved
And that everything is going to be OK.

When?

When will the tears stop falling?
When will death stop feeling so welcoming?
When will my broken wings heal?
Will love I ever feel?

Burning Flame

Look into my eyes, my soul.
There you will see
The burning flame,
Deep inside of me.

A raging fire
Of love, strength, and beauty.
So long tamed,
But now wild and free.

Look closely
And see the fire behind my eyes
That sometimes flickers,
But never dies.

Troubled Waters

So much hatred pours down on her.
Like a rain shower.
But she doesn't drown because of a higher power.
He keeps her head above the water and His gentle hands push her further and further.
And when she gets tired of the negativity,
She hears a voice whisper, "It is OK my child, rest on me.
I won't ever allow you to succumb to the turmoil of the black sea.
When life becomes too much, I will become your mind, soul, and body.
Don't surrender to the negativity.
Come to me.
You are mine and I love you.
I will always help you through."

The Other You

On the outside, so beautiful and strong.
But on the inside, there are pieces broken.
Pain buried behind a secret door.
You don't allow too many in.
People judge,
Don't know who you really are.
You have insecurities,
Even though you are a superstar.

Mirror, Mirror

Am I beautiful, beautiful, beautiful?
I questioned myself every day.
"Make me beautiful, beautiful, beautiful,"
To God I would pray.
When I looked in the mirror,
Names bullies would call me, would be all I could see.
When I looked in the mirror,
Could only see the vitiligo on my body.
When I stared in the mirror,
I saw a lost soul filled with emptiness,
Allowing men to abuse her,
Because she felt valueless.
Shy, ugly, and broken.
I didn't believe I deserved better.
Then one day, God brought a special man into my life.
Who changed my life forever.
He said I was beautiful, beautiful, beautiful.
Not the broken woman I saw staring at me in the mirror.
He made me stare back at her,
Until I slowly began to fall in love with her.

He told me people who mock and hate others are insecure people.
They are jealous and envy other people's greatness.
His words and love helped me begin to heal from within.
I believed that I, too, deserved a life of happiness.
Now when I look into the mirror I smile.
I see beauty.
Now when I look into the mirror,
I see and embrace me.
I am beautiful, beautiful, beautiful.
I say every day,
"I am worthy, worthy, worthy."
I thank God for helping me find my way.

The Past

My past is the past.
It is a part of my history.

Living in the present,
But my past will always be a part of me.

Not looking back, only towards the future.
Not ashamed of yesterday.

It is because of yesterday
That I am stronger and wiser today.

Bruised, not Broken

With greatness
Comes mockery.

Words have cut.
My heart has bled.

I hurt.
Hurt a lot.

Bruised I am.
Broken I am not.

If People Knew Me

People think they know,
But do they really know?

For if they truly knew,
Would they hurt me so?

Would they finally accept me?
Accept me for me?

Or would they continue to try to change me
Into the person they think I should be?

If they really knew,
Really knew me,

I wonder,
Would there be so much hate and mockery?

He Saved Me

For so long I thought it was impossible for anyone to love me.
The value of my worth I could not see.
Didn't feel worthy of anyone's love.
Only saw black clouds when I looked up at the sky above.
Down the path of darkness, I walked further and further,
Until I thought I would be lost forever.
Then one day, when completely broken, wishing for my life to be over,
I found myself falling to my knees, crying out to my Heavenly Father.
From the ground He lifted me and showed me the way.
I still give thanks to Him today.
He placed scriptures inside of my heart.
Psalms 30:5 keeps me from falling apart.

Accept Me

Will you accept me?
Accept me for me?
And not the woman you think I am on TV.

Will you accept me?
Accept me for me?
And not try to change me into the woman you want me to be.

Will you accept me?
Accept me for me?
Will you love me?

Will you?

And will you understand,
I am more than just a celebrity?

I Dance

When the sky darkens
And dark clouds hover above me,
I stretch my arms and dance in the shadows.
Like it is spring and I'm barefoot in the meadows.
I hear thunder.
Like a drum beat.
A beat
That guides my feet.
Beneath the darkened skies,
I stretch my arms and dance in the shadows
Like it is spring and I'm barefoot in the meadows.
I am a ray of sunshine
In a world of darkness.
No matter how bad the storm gets,
The rain can never wash away my happiness.

She Wears a Smile

Sometimes the pain
Aches so deep.
Didn't know nightmares came
When not even asleep.
Frightened little girl inside
Wants to run and hide.
But the woman smiles to the world,
Hiding the tears she has cried.
Old wounds are bandaged
But never completely healed.
A beautiful smile she wears
As her only shield.

Judge Me Not

Judge me not,
When your heart is as dark as midnight.
Judge me not,
When you have taken more left turns than right.
Judge me not,
With skeletons filling up your closet.
Judge me not,
For refusing to be your puppet.
Judge me not,
For you are not my master.
Judge me not,
For I answer to a Higher Power.
Judge me not,
For God is my creator.
Judge me not,
For He is my Master, Judge, and Father.
So, judge me not,
For following and obeying Him only
And not being what you think I should be.
So, judge me not.
You cannot convict me,
For you are only human.
God is the only one with the key to Eternity.

Bruises Fade

Bruises fade but remain
On the heart like a stain,
Spilling memories of abuse from the past.
Seeing myself lying there, wondering how long
beatings would last.
Each time thinking I would never survive.
Today feel so blessed to be alive.
And though I am stronger and stronger each day,
The past never goes away.
I am and will always be free,
But the pain in my heart forever lives in me.

When I Think of Him

Memories of the past
Still make tears fall.
Thinking of him
Makes me feel less than five feet tall.
And I find myself reliving those moments
And feeling like the lost, scared woman I was back then.
Making me wonder to myself after all these years,
Have I truly healed or just buried the pain deep within?

What Would You Say?

If you could, what would you tell the man who beat you down?
The one who took your heart and stamped it on the ground.
To the man who told you that you were nothing,
The one who caused you so much pain and suffering,
That made you feel so much misery,
You thought by his hands or your own that you'd end up in a cemetery.
The man that took away your self-value
Until you couldn't even love yourself.
This monster,
Who made himself feel powerful, by making you weaker.
If you had the chance to confront him today,
What would you say?

To My Younger Self

I see you crying
And I am crying with you.
I'm throwing you a rope
To pull you through.
You're in the midst of the storm,
But I have made it over the rainbow.
Your pot of gold awaits you,
So, hold on and don't let go.
You've got to have faith,
Even in the midst of bad weather.
The dark clouds will part.
The storm will not last forever.
So, hold on.
Don't let go.
I am your Future.
And I am waiting for you on the other side of the rainbow.

Baggage

In a corner sits my baggage,
And it remains there day after day.
People tell me it's no good.
I need to throw it away.
And I tell them,
If they stop looking at baggage in a negative way,
They will see how special it is
And why I treasure it rather than throw it away.
My baggage is more than just baggage.
It is filled with emotions and memories of yesterday.
That is why I choose to hold onto it
And not throw it away.
It may weight a lot,
But it does not hold me down.
It actually steadies me,
Keeps my feet on solid ground.
I look at this baggage
And it reminds me
Of how far I've come to being who I am today.
And how it didn't kill me, but made me stronger.
So, to you this may just be baggage,
But to me it is my life story.
And who and where would I be,

Without my history?

I'm Real

My smile is real.
Not painted on.

My heart is tender.
Not made of stone.

Strong but fragile.
So, handle me gently.

If you can't love me.
Please, don't hurt me.

Words of Wisdom

My mama once told me
If a man can't treat me like a lady
Then to keep on moving.
Don't waste my time crying.
I'm not a punching bag,
Or a price tag.
I am a lady.
And that's how a man should treat me.
My mama once told me
That love isn't easy.
And it never will be.
Love is very complicated,
But don't be afraid to grab hold of it.
She said never settle for anything.
Because I am tired of searching.
Patience is the key
To finding the man who'll treat me like a lady.

Reflection

How I feel on the inside,
For years I have tried to hide.
But one glance in the mirror
Will cause my whole world to shatter.
My eyes only reveal self-destruction,
Making me afraid of my reflection.
I feel so sad and alone.
Just barely hanging on.
I face each day,
Feeling like a part of me is slipping away.
And the only way I can keep it together
Is by avoiding a mirror.

I Am a Woman

You must think I am a punching bag,
Because you constantly hit me.
You must think I am a price tag,
Because you're always trying to buy my love and affection.
You must think I am a door mat,
Because you try to walk all over me.
You must think I am a cat,
Because you act like you own me.
It is clear that you do not see me as a human being
But as some worthless object.
I am a woman.
It's time you realize it.

You Don't Know Me

I've opened up my soul,
So the world can see
Even nice and intelligent girls' lives
Are filled with misery.
So, don't think you know me
By simply what you see.
I may be intelligent and friendly,
But on the inside, I'm sad and lonely.

My Guidance

The road ahead is so cloudy
That I cannot see.
But I walk slowly,
Because God is watching over me.
He will guide me
And lead me across safely.
My faith in Him is strong.
I know His love is what keeps me moving along.

Going to Make It

I am going to climb the wall
And pray that I do not fall.
But if I do,
I promise you
I will stand
And try again.
And if I keep falling,
I will stand and continue climbing.
For some day,
I will make it all the way.

Why Do We Love People?

Let me tell you a story,
About a man I once knew.
(Yes, baby, I'm about to talk
about you.)
Just saw me as a friend
He knew right way back then.
Never spoke the truth.
Just kept stringing me along.
Would never call me,
Unless in need.
(Oh, baby, you had to stick me deep,
See me bleed.)
Never did things
Said he would do.
(Oh, baby, why
Did I have to fall for you?)
This man set my heart on fire,
Then slowly watched it burn.
Why do we love people,
Who do not love us in return?

Lost

When we met,
I forgot about my own life.
My focus was becoming your girlfriend
And hopefully one day your wife.
Forgot about taking care of me,
But focused on what would make you happy.
The things you always desired,
I tried to be.
What you wanted.
The woman you searched for.
I tried to be that woman
And much more.
Who I was,
Was lost and forgotten.
Then came the dreaded words,
"Let's just be friends."
Now you are gone
And so am I.
I traded my identity
For the love of a guy.

You Are so Beautiful

Do you know
How beautiful you are?
How your eyes sparkle
Like a shooting star,
Landing into the hearts
Of the young and old?
Do you know
You are a beauty to behold?
Your smile, your laugh
Illuminate any room that you enter.
Becoming the sunshine
To one's stormy weather.
You are loved and adored.
Treasured like a precious ruby.
When looking in the mirror,
I hope you will always see
The beautiful, strong, and courageous
Woman that I and others see.

Odd Girl Out

It makes me uncomfortable
To have people staring at me.
Because I know
That they are seeing something ugly.
All my life
I've been told I'm not pretty.
So, I know what strangers say
When they look at me.
Odd girl out.
So alone I am.
But I am human with a heart.
And it hurts no one gives a damn!

Perfection She Never Claimed to Be

Perfection she has never claimed to be,
But if you look with your heart and not your eyes,
A beautiful, strong woman you will see.
She is a beauty to behold,
For through her eyes,
Shines a heart of gold.
Her approach to life
Is to walk in the light of God,
Making her an extraordinary friend, mother, and wife.
People may not understand
Why she doesn't fall when they throw stones,
But God has her by the hand.
He shields and protects her,
For even though she smiles,
God knows she carries the weight of the world on her shoulders.

Trying to Live

Trying to live right in a world of wrong,
In search of a place to belong.
On the outside looking in,
I am my only friend.
Peace not here or there,
Hatred is everywhere.
At a crossroad with no map,
Running towards or from the Devil's lap.
Free and a prisoner,
A Christian, and a sinner;
Confused and lost
In a world where freedom costs.

Silence

Buried feelings.
The resurrection of a monster.
Revenge and pain
Feeds its hunger.
Blinded
By rage.
Encaged
Within the rampage.
Speaks your heart.
Sets you free.
Silence.
The imprisonment of your own captivity.

Behind the Mask

It is time to stop masquerading
And reveal the person from within.
A person who appears strong,
But does not have steel for skin.
To finally let people see the truth
When they throw stone after stone.
To be hit constantly
Does not break a bone….
It chips away at my heart,
Until it completely breaks apart.
Maybe the stone throwers will stop
If they finally see my bleeding heart.
So, I am stopping my masquerading
And revealing the person within.
I appear strong,
But I do not have steel for skin.

Who Are We

We have all asked ourselves who are we,
But how do we really know the answer?
Do we really know our identity?
Is who we are
Defined by our own definition?
Can we really say who we are,
Without any hesitation?
Or is who we are
What others told us to be?
Leaving the question how authentic are we,
Being a carbon copy of someone else's destiny.
Is the person we say we are
Truly the person we are from within?
Or have we been wearing masks for so long,
That our masks have come to look and feel genuine?
Leaving us to believe
We are truthful defining our identity.
So, I end with this question for you:
Who are you really?

Need of Love

Because she was always told that she wasn't important,
She grew up searching for a sense of value elsewhere.
Her vulnerability left her open.
She just wanted someone to care.
"You're beautiful. You're special."
Words she so longed to hear.
She fell in love with the first man
Who whispered them into her ear.
But she was more in love with the message
Rather than the messenger,
Because of the deep void
Of what she longed to hear.
Never realizing she was being dehumanized
More and more each day.
For while she thought she was feeling love,
Pieces of her were being chipped away.
She became a doormat,
Stepped upon so much until she was broken.
Purple and blue
Were now the colors of her skin.
And after he had enough

Of using her as a punching bag,
She was tossed aside,
Like a used piece of rag.
Leaving her with the emptiness she once felt.
But now bigger, darker, and deeper than ever.
Allowing her to willingly surrender
To the next man who will approach her.
And the cycle will continue,
Over and over and over again.
Because of her need
To fill a bottomless hole that lies within.

Lost and Confused

Will I see another day?
Feel my life slipping away.
There is a part of me that wants to die,
But ashamed my death will embarrass my family.
There is a part of me that wants to live,
But living means bruises as my reality.
So lost and confused.
Want to be free.
Don't know which world to turn to.
Who will rescue me?

Lost Now Found

I was lost but now found.
Finally, am free.
But still find myself running
From the demons chasing me.
Wanting to capture and drag me back,
Into a time of darkness.
But I am stronger, wiser, and know who I am.
I know I deserve happiness.
So, I run, run, run, and run,
Never looking back or slowing down.
I am a queen
And won't allow these demons to take my crown.

She Fell in Love with a Man

She fell in love with a man
Whose fist was as hard as his heart was of stone.
Who acted like a hungry dog
And saw her as nothing more than a bone.
His ego being pleasured and pleased
Was all that mattered.
So, all of her dreams,
He took and shattered.
Because of his own insecurities,
He took his pain out on her.
Weakening her
In order for him to feel stronger.
He knew
She was a lost soul,
So, he wanted her,
Just to control.
Not man enough
To carry the weight on his own,
So, upon her shoulders,
He placed the heavy stone.
He needed her
To escape his insecurity.

He wanted to feel the glow,
Radiating from her beauty.
He wanted her heart
To take as his own.
To feel alive,
Since his was made of stone.
He loved not her,
But loved more of himself.
So, he made her bottle up her emotions
And put them away on a shelf.
For she was beauty.
He, the beast.
And her self-worth
Was his feast.

He Loves Me

I love my Heavenly Father
And I know He loves me.
He has been my eyes
When I could not see.
He has been my voice
When I could not speak.
He has been my legs
When I could not walk.
He has been my everything.
My life saver.

Help Me

The words are there in the depths of my soul,
Swimming around and around in my head.
But the passageway leading to my mouth
It cannot seem to find.
HELP ME!!

I am screaming for help,
But no one hears.
I am crying.
No one sees my tears.

HELP ME!!
SOMEBODY!!
ANYBODY!!
PLEASE.... HELP ME!!

The Darkness

I lie awake at night
And cry into the darkness.
Only the darkness knows and understands
My sadness.
My loneliness.
Embracing me.
Knowing what I am longing.
And it is darkness that soothes my pain
And keeps me from crumbling,
Crumbling into dust.
Making darkness my only friend,
The only one to trust
In a world that treats me like I do not exist.

See Me

You see.
And you hear me.
Do not look away.
You know I am not OK.
When you hear.
And when you see.
Please, I'm begging you.
Help me.
I am not OK.
I am not OK.
Ignoring me.
Will not make Domestic Violence go away.

One Day

One day the abuse will end
And I will not be broken.
My name will not be on a wreath.
The ground my body will not be beneath.
One day I will find the courage and say,
"No More!"
And walk out the door.

Wallflower Child

Why am I so hated?
So unloved?
So unappreciated?
What's wrong with me?
What's wrong with me?
What's wrong with me?
There must be something wrong with me….

Escape

How do you escape abuse
When you can't tell anyone what's going on?
When your heart is so tender,
But shielded within a stone,
How do you escape abuse?
When no one believes you,
Because the abuse isn't physical but emotional
And bodies are not see-through.
And you smile,
Though your smile is plastic,
Where your pain hides behind.
Because you are afraid.
What will happen when your secret will no longer be a secret?

Love Me or Leave Me

Treat me right.
Don't treat me wrong.

Love me or leave me.
Don't make me a country song.

The Fear

I will not raise my hand.
I will not stand.
I do not want to stay.
I cannot walk away.
I cannot tell family or a friend.
I want it to end.
I fear what will happen
If the truth is spoken.
Isolated me from friends and family.
No one would believe me.
Am I to blame?
I am filled with so much shame.
I am too broken.
The truth cannot be spoken.
Will I be judged instead of rescued?
Is staying accepting to be abused?
I am afraid, ashamed, and confused.
I do not want to be abused.
I want it to end,
But I am too broken to know where to begin.
I do not want to stay.
I am too afraid to walk away.

Before It's Physical

Before it's physical,
It's emotional and mental.
He hurts you from the inside,
Before abusing you physically.
Once psychologically damaged,
Under his control,
He can now physically beat you,
Since he has already killed your soul.

Black Butterfly

A butterfly cries....
But never dies.
Even after it's gone,
Its spirit lives on.
So, spread your wings and fly.
You will never die, Butterfly.

The Son, the Father

To the Son, the Father,
I bow down unto you.
You died and have risen.
Cleanse my soul and make me anew.

You Don't Love Me

I keep loving you,
Hoping one day you will again love me, too.
Cover my body with tender kisses
Instead of bruises.
I want to hear the words, "I love you," and feel loved too,
Instead of feeling fear in the presence of you.
I miss the man I once knew.
The man I loved and who loved me, too.

Unbreakable

Bruised and battered,
But my spirit not shattered.
You placed in me fear,
With pain behind every tear.
But each time I became broken,
God made me whole again.
Until unbreakable I became.
No more fear or shame.
Now with strength and clarity,
I have broken free.

Rainbow Spirit

In the darkness,
A Rainbow you became.
No more hiding behind sunglasses.
No more feelings of shame.

You entered darkness and stepped out a Rainbow.
Becoming strength for the weak.
A voice to others
Who are still afraid to speak.

In your darkness,
You became a Rainbow.
No more hiding.
Now a light for others to follow.

Let Go

Say goodbye to the old you
And say hello to the new.
You are God's child,
And He has something special for you.
You made it through the storm.
Now enjoy the rainbow.
Inhale the fresh air.
Let the past go.

You Can Do It

It is going to be hard.
But you can do it.

BELIEVE.

Take a deep breath.
Relax your mind.

LEAVE.

Until It's Too Late

What are you thinking?
What is your smile hiding?
What is your sleeve covering?
Are your nights spent crying?
Are you in pain and sorrow?
Don't let the monster take away your tomorrow.

Call Now

Do not take pills.
Do not end your life.
Put down the gun.
Let go of the knife.
Do not take your final breath.
This is not the way.
You are tired, I understand.
But you are going to be OK.
Don't jump or crash.
Don't drown in alcohol.
That National Domestic Violence Hotline number is
1-800-799-7233.
They are waiting for you to call.

One Day at a Time

One day at a time,
I'm putting my life back together.
One day at a time,
I am becoming stronger.
Not looking back,
Only the future I see.
A place of happiness.
A place where I am free.

Stronger

Many, many times,
She stood face to face with death.
And even though frightened,
She did not allow death to take her final breath.

He smiled every time she fell,
Thinking he had broken her.
But soon learned pain didn't kill her.
It only made her stronger.

Life is Beautiful

I never knew how much I was dying
Until I began living.
My soul had gone into hiding
But now has come a spiritual awakening.

I am beautiful.
I feel beautiful.
Life is beautiful.

Let us not Forget

Let us not forget
The ones no longer here.
The ones who suffered in silence
And lived in fear.
These beautiful, strong women,
Who have been forever silenced.
Let their memory forever shine bright
And give us strength as we continue to fight
Domestic Violence.

Beautiful, Strong Woman

Regardless of what you've been told,
You are a beauty to behold.
Do not listen to lies told by your man,
For you are a Beautiful, Strong Woman.
You deserve to be treated with love and respect,
But the longer you stay, you won't get it.
It's time you take a stand.
Leave your abusive husband.
There's a better world you can find,
But you must leave this abusive world behind.
Being on your own may seem scary,
But at least you'll be free.
Just have courage and believe.
You have no choice but to leave.
And you can.
Because you are a Beautiful, Strong Woman.
And you can do whatever you set your mind to.
Even leaving the man hurting you.

Rise Up!

Rise Up!
Stand!
Your value is not determined
By the love of a man.
You are worthy!
You are beauty!

Rise Up!
Stand!
Your value is not determined
By the love of a man.

You are courageous!
You are strong!
In an abusive relationship,
You do not belong!

Rise Up!
Stand!
Your value is not determined
By the love of a man!

You are precious!
You are priceless!

Allow no man
To steal your happiness.

Rise Up!
Stand!
Your value is not determined
By the love of a man.

You are SOMEBODY!
You are SOMEBODY!
You are SOMEBODY!

You are a Beautiful, Strong Woman.
Allow no man to take your identity.

So, rise up!
Stand!
Your value is not determined
By the love of a man.

Sisters United

We are sisters united.
Together we stand tall.
Violence against one
Is violence against us all.

We are strength,
To those who are weak.
The voice,
To those unable to speak.

We are sisters united.
Together we stand tall.
Violence against one
Is violence against us all.

We are….

The Girl Power Movement.
The Tell Your Truth Movement.
The Women Empowering Other Women Movement.
The #Metoo Movement.
The Time Is Up Movement.

We are women saying….

No, to sexual abuse.
No, to harassment.
No, to all forms of violence.

We will not be silenced!

We are sisters united.
When one falls, we all fall.
But when we stand together….

WE WILL RISE ABOVE IT ALL!

Contact the Author

Reviews are so important to an author so I'd appreciate it if you could put a review on Amazon please. If you'd like to contact me, please do so via:

Email: poetryfanbox@gmail.com

Twitter: @thankfulpoet

Facebook: Kimberly Hockaday

I look forward to hearing from you.

Kimberly

Acknowledgments

I would like to thank everyone who helped me in the making of this book and especially my former seventh grade teacher, Mrs. Marie Robinson, for proofreading my manuscript, and my publisher, Jacky Donovan, for seeing my book worthy of publication and helping me in the process of getting it published.

Further Books from the Author

Kimberly Hockaday is the author of further poetry books which are available on Amazon:

A Mourner's Diary: Poems of Grief and Healing

Soul Mates: Poems of Eternal Love

About the Author

Kimberly Hockaday is a poet and author from Roanoke Rapids, North Carolina, and is a Distinguished Student Poet of Eastern North Carolina. She created a monthly poetry reading gathering called Poetry Reading Extravaganza in 2013 and has had her works published in newspapers and literary magazines.

Kimberly is a former contributor to *Real Hot Magazine* and has performed at a number of venues including Art Out Loud in Roanoke Rapids and the Juneteenth Celebrations in Garysburg, North Carolina. She is passionate about the arts and enjoys writing poetry with a purpose. She hopes her writing not only entertains but also educates and inspires her readers.

State Coalitions

Alabama Coalition Against Domestic Violence
P. O. Box 4762
Montgomery, AL 36101
Hotline: 1 (800) 650-6522
Office: (334) 832-4842 Fax: (334) 832-4803
Website: www.acadv.org
Email: info@acadv.org

Alaska Network on Domestic Violence & Sexual Assault
130 Seward Street, Suite 214
Juneau, AK 99801
Office: (907) 586-3650
Website: www.andvsa.org
Email: andvsa@andvsa.org

Arizona Coalition Against Domestic Violence
2800 N. Central Ave., Suite 1570
Phoenix, AZ 85004
Hotline: 1 (800) 782-6400
Office: (602) 279-2900 Fax: (602) 279-2980
Website: www.azcadv.org
Email: info@azcadv.org

Arkansas Coalition Against Domestic Violence
1401 W. Capitol Avenue, Suite 170
Little Rock, AR 72201
Hotline: 1 (800) 269-4668
Office: (501) 907-5612 Fax: (501) 907-5618
Website: www.domesticpeace.com
California Partnership to End Domestic Violence
P. O. Box 1798
Sacramento, CA 95812
Hotline: 1 (800) 524-4765
Office: (916) 444-7163 Fax: (916) 444-7165
Website: www.cpedv.org
Email: info@cpedv.org

Colorado Coalition Against Domestic Violence
1120 Lincoln St, #900
Denver, CO 80203
Office: (303) 831-9632
Website: www.ccadv.org

Connecticut Coalition Against Domestic Violence
912 Silas Deane Highway, Lower Level
Wethersfield, CT 06109
Hotline: (888) 774-2900
Office: (860) 282-7899 Fax: (860) 282-7892
Website: www.ctcadv.org

Delaware Coalition Against Domestic Violence
100 W. 10th Street, Suite 903
Wilmington, DE 19801
Northern Delaware: (302) 762-6110
Southern Delaware: (302) 422-8058 Bilingual: (302) 745-9874
Office: (302) 658-2958
Website: www.dcadv.org

DC Coalition Against Domestic Violence
5 Thomas Circle, NW
Washington, DC 20005
Office: (202) 299-1181 Fax: (202) 299-1193
Website: www.dccadv.org
Email: info@dccadv.org

Florida Coalition Against Domestic Violence
425 Office Plaza
Tallahassee, FL 32301
Hotline: (800) 500-1119
TDD: (850) 621-4202
Office: (850) 425-2749 Fax: (850) 425-3091
Website: www.fcadv.org

Georgia Coalition Against Domestic Violence
114 New Street, Suite B
Decatur, GA 30030
Hotline: 1 (800) 334-2836
Office: (404) 209-0280 Fax: (404) 766-3800
Website: www.gcadv.org

Guam Coalition Against Sexual Assault & Family Violence
P.O. Box 1093
Hagatna, GU 96932
Office: (671) 479-2277 Fax: (671) 479-7233
Website: www.guamcoalition.org
Email: info@guamcoalition.org

Hawaii State Coalition Against Domestic Violence
810 Richards Street, Suite 960
Honolulu, HI 96813
Office: (808) 832-9316 Fax: (808) 841-6028

Website: www.hscadv.org

Idaho Coalition Against Sexual & Domestic Violence
300 E. Mallard Drive, Suite 130
Boise, ID 83706
Office: (208) 384-0419
Website: www.idvsa.org
Email: info@engagingvoices.org

Illinois Coalition Against Domestic Violence
Hotline: (877) 863-6338
Office: (217) 789-2830
Website: www.ilcadv.org

Indiana Coalition Against Domestic Violence
1915 W. 18th Street, Suite B
Indianapolis, IN 46202
Hotline: 1 (800) 332-7385
Office: (317) 917-3685 Fax: (317) 917-3695
Website: www.icadvinc.org

Iowa Coalition against Domestic Violence
3030 Merle Hay Road
Des Moines, IA 50310
Hotline: 1 (800) 942-0333
Office: (515) 244-8028 Fax: (515) 244-7417
Website: www.icadv.org
Email: icadv@icadv.org

Kansas Coalition against Sexual & Domestic Violence
634 SW Harrison Street
Topeka, KS 66603
Hotline: 1 (888) 363-2287
Office: (785) 232-9784 Fax: (785) 266-1874

Website: www.kcsdv.org

Kentucky Domestic Violence Association
111 Darby Shire Circle
Frankfort, KY 40601
Office: (502) 209-5382 Fax: (502) 226-5382
Website: www.kdva.org
Email: info@kdva.org

Louisiana Coalition Against Domestic Violence
P.O. Box 77308
Baton Rouge, LA 70879
Hotline: 1 (888) 411-1333
Office: (225) 752-1296
Website: www.lcadv.org

Maine Coalition to End Domestic Violence
One Weston Court, Box#2
Augusta, ME 04330
Hotline: 1 (866) 834-4357
Office: (207) 430-8334 Fax: (207) 430-8348
Website: www.mcedv.org
Email: info@mcedv.org

Maryland Network Against Domestic Violence
4601 Presidents Dr., Ste. 370
Lanham, MD 20706
Hotline: 1 (800) 634-3577
Office: (301) 429-3601 Fax: (301) 429-3605
Website: www.mnadv.org
Email: info@mnadv.org

Massachusetts Coalition Against Sexual Assault &
Domestic Violence/Jane Doe, Inc.
14 Beacon Street, Suite 507

Boston, MA 02108
Hotline: 1 (877) 785-2020
TTY/TTD: 1 (877) 521-2601
Office: (617) 248-0922 Fax: (617) 248-0902
Website: www.janedoe.org
Email: info@janedoe.org

Michigan Coalition to End Domestic & Sexual Violence
3893 Okemos Road, Suite B2
Okemos, MI 48864
Office: (517) 347-7000 Fax: (517) 347-1377
TTY: (517) 381-8470
Website: www.mcedsv.org

Minnesota Coalition for Battered Women
60 Plato Blvd. E, Suite 130
Saint Paul, MN 55107
Hotline: 1 (866) 223-1111
Office: (651) 646-6177 Fax: (651) 646-1527
Website: www.mcbw.org

Mississippi Coalition Against Domestic Violence
P.O. Box 4703
Jackson, MS 39296
Hotline: 1 (800) 898-3234
Office: (601) 981-9196 Fax: (601) 981-2501
Website: www.mcadv.org
Email: support@mcadv.org

Missouri Coalition Against Domestic & Sexual Violence
217 Oscar Dr., Suite A
Jefferson City, MO 65101
Office: (573) 634-4161
Website: www.mocadsv.org

Montana Coalition Against Domestic & Sexual Violence
32 S Ewing St
Helena, MT 59601
Office: (406) 443-7794
Website: www.mcadsv.com
Email: mtcoalition@mcadsv.com

Nebraska Domestic Violence Sexual Assault Coalition
245 South 84th St, Suite 200
Lincoln, NE 68510
Office: (402) 476-6256 Fax: (402) 476-6806
Spanish Hotline: (877) 215-0167
Website: www.ndvsac.org

Nevada Network Against Domestic Violence
250 South Rock Bldvd., Suite 116
Reno, NV 89502
(775) 828-1115 Fax: (775) 828-9911
Website: www.nnadv.org

New Hampshire Coalition Against Domestic & Sexual Violence
P.O. Box 353
Concord, NH 03302
Hotline: 1 (866) 644-3574
Office: (603) 224-8893 Fax: (603) 228-6096
Website: www.nhcadsv.org

New Jersey Coalition for Battered Women
1670 Whitehorse Hamilton Square
Trenton, NJ 08690
Hotline: 1 (800) 572-7233 TTY: (800) 787-3224

Office: (609) 584-8107 Fax: (609) 584-9750
Website: www.njcbw.org

New Mexico Coalition Against Domestic Violence
1210 Luisa Street, Suite 7
Santa Fe, NM 87505
Office: (505) 246-9240 Fax: (505) 246-9240
Website: www.nmcadv.org
Email: info@nmcadv.org

New York State Coalition Against Domestic Violence
119 Washington Avenue, 3rd Floor
Albany, NY 12210
Hotline NYS: 1 (800) 942-6906
Hotline NYC: 1 (800) 621-4673
Office: (518) 482-5465 Fax: (518) 482-3807
Website: www.nyscadv.org

North Carolina Coalition Against Domestic Violence
3710 University Drive, Suite 140
Durham, NC 27707
Office: (919) 956-9124 Fax: (919) 682-1449
Website: www.nccadv.org

North Dakota Council on Abused Women's Services
525 N. 4th St.
Bismark, ND 58501
Office: (701) 255-6240 Fax: (701) 255-1904
Website: www.ndcaws.org

Ohio Domestic Violence Network
Hotline: (800) 934-9840
Website: www.odvn.org

Oklahoma Coalition Against Domestic Violence &
Sexual Assault
3815 N. Santa Fe Ave., Suite 124
Oklahoma City, OK 73118
Hotline: 1 (800) 522-7233
Office: (405) 524-0700 TTY: (405) 512-5577
Website: www.ocadvsa.org
Email: info@ocadvsa.org

Oregon Coalition Against Domestic & Sexual
Violence
9570 SW Barbur Blvd., Suite 214
Portland, OR 97219
Hotline: 1 (888) 235-5333
Office: (503) 230-1951 Fax: (503) 230-1973
Website: www.ocadsv.org

Pennsylvania Coalition Against Domestic Violence
3605 Vartan Way, Suite 101
Harrisburg PA 17110
Office (717) 545-6400 TTY (800) 553-2508
Website: www.pcadv.org

Coordinadora Paz para la Mujer
Apartado 193008
San Juan, Puerto Rico 00919-3008
Office: (787) 281-7579
Website: ww.pazparalamujer.org
Email: pplmsmtp@ayustar.net

Rhode Island Coalition Against Domestic Violence
422 Post Road, Suite 201
Warwick, RI 02888
Hotline: 1 (800) 494-8100
Office: (401) 467-9940 Fax: (401) 467-9943

Website: www.ricadv.org
Email: ricadv@ricadv.org

South Carolina Coalition Against Domestic Violence & Sexual Assault
P.O. Box 7776
Columbia, SC 29202
Office: (803) 256-2900
Website: www.sccadvasa.org

South Dakota Coalition Ending Domestic Violence & Sexual Assault
P.O. Box 141
Pierre, SD 57501
Office: (605) 945-0869
Website: www.sdcedsv.org

Tennessee Coalition to End Domestic & Sexual Violence
2 International Plaza Dr. Suite 425
Nashville, TN 37217
Hotline: 1 (800) 356-6767
Office: (615) 386-9406
Website: tncoalition.org

Texas Council on Family Violence
P.O. Box 163865
Austin, TX 78716
Office: (512) 794-1133 Fax: (512) 685.6397
Website: www.tcfv.org

Women's Coalition of St. Croix
P.O. Box 222734
Christiansted, VI 00822-2734
Hotline: (340) 773-9272

Fax: (340) 773-9062
Website: www.wcstx.com
Email: info@wcstx.org

Utah Domestic Violence Coalition
205 North 400 West,
Salt Lake City, UT 84103
Hotline: 1 (800) 897-5465
Office: (801) 521-5544
Website: www.udvc.org

Vermont Network Against Domestic & Sexual Violence
P.O. Box 405
Montpelier, VT 05601
Hotline: 1 (800) 228-7395
Office: (802) 223-1302 Fax: (802) 223-6943
Website: www.vtnetwork.org
Email: vtnetwork@vtnetwork.org

Virginia Sexual & Domestic Violence Action Alliance
5008 Monument Avenue, Suite A
Richmond, VA 23230
Office: (804) 377-0335
Website: www.vsdvalliance.org
Email: info@vsdvalliance.org

Washington State Coalition Against Domestic Violence
711 Capitol Way, Suite 702
Olympia, WA 98501
Hotline: 1 (800) 562-6025
Office: (360) 586-1022 Fax: (360) 586-1024
Website: www.wscadv.org

Email: wscadv@wscadv.org

West Virginia Coalition Against Domestic Violence
5004 Elk River Road, South
Elkview, WV 25071
Office: (304) 965-3552 Fax: (304) 965-3572
Website: www.wvcadv.org

Wisconsin Coalition Against Domestic Violence
1245 E. Washington Ave, Suite 150
Madison, WI 53703
Office: (608) 255-0539 Fax: (608) 255-3560
Website: endabusewi.org
Email: wcadv@wcadv.org

Wyoming Coalition Against Domestic Violence & Sexual Assault
P.O. Box 236
710 Garfield Street, Suite 218
Laramie, WY 82073
Office: (307) 755-5481 Fax: (307) 755-5482
Website: www.wyomingdvsa.org

Made in the USA
Columbia, SC
10 November 2023